T0107143

THE INCOGNITO BODY

The Incognito Body

poems by

Cynthia Hogue

RED HEN PRESS ✹ LOS ANGELES

The Incognito Body

Cover art: "Woman on the Beach," mixed media by Julia Ball
Author's Photo: Sylvain Gallais

Book design by Michael Vukadinovich
Cover Design by Mark E. Cull

ISBN: 1-59709-021-2
Library of Congress Catalog Card Number: 2005932927

Red Hen Press www.redhen.org

The City of Los Angeles Cultural Affairs Department, California Arts Council, Los Angeles County Arts Commission and National Endowment for the Arts partially support Red Hen Press.

First Edition

Acknowledgments

Grateful acknowledgment is made to the editors of the journals in which some of these poems first appeared (some in earlier versions and under different titles): 42 Opus: "The Seeker"; Antioch Review: "psalm: wakefulness," "Stones,"; "Till I Have Conquered in Myself What Causes War"; Ars Interpres: "She forecast the future"; Artful Dodge: "High Tea with Virginia"; Barrow Street: "Interior," "Once Upon a Time," "psalm: at the retreat house"; Connecticut Review: "Elegy," "psalm: after hiking reading the stars"; Emily Dickinson International Society Bulletin: "Honesty"; Electronic Poetry Review: "In Distrust of Good"; Hayden's Ferry: "Though We Change, One Flying after Another," "It Is True That the True Appearance of an Object," "A Poem with Lines from Elytis' Eros, Eros, Eros"; Hotel Amerika: "The Book of What Is," "Have We After All Come To"; How(ever)2: "The Incognito Body"; New Orleans Review: "Seeing Northern Lights on Taos Mesa"; Nidus: "Elemental Attention. Stillness"; Notre Dame Review: "Memory Y," "At Delphi"; 42 Opus: "The Seeker"; Poetry International: "Body Scans," "In a Mute Season," "Radical Optimism," "Shame"; Salt River Review: "Late Nights with Albert," "Resurrection Is a Sense of Direction," "That Wild Chance of Living"; Spoon River Poetry Review: "The Sibyl's Spring"; The Journal: "Four Ways of Seeing the Fall"; Volt: "Modern Life."

"Till I Have Conquered in Myself What Causes War" and "In a Mute Season" were reprinted as part of the monthly "featured poet" section in the electronic journal PoetryMagazine (February 2002). "Elemental Attention. Stillness" was chosen as the Web Monthly Feature for May, 2003 on Verse Daily. "The Book of What Is" was featured on Poetry Daily (July 11, 2004), as part of the feature on Hotel Amerika, and nominated for a Pushcart Prize. "Honesty" was part of an EDIS Bulletin annual feature, "Poet to Poet," one contemporary poet and Emily Dickinson (2005).

Thanks to The Helene Wurlitzer Foundation of New Mexico for support while I wrote some of the poems in this book, and to the Stadler Center for Poetry and Bucknell University for the sabbatical time that enabled me to complete the collection and for time at Breadloaf. As ever, abiding gratitude to writer-friends who have helped me along the way: Aliki Barnstone, Paula Closson Buck, Charles Borkhuis, Monifa Love, Adrian Oktenberg, Karl Patten, Jeannine Savard, Pamela Stewart, and Dean Stover. Deep thanks to Norman Dubie, Kathleen Fraser, Alberto Rios, Peggy Shumaker and Afaa Weaver, for their help at crucial times. And to my dear husband, Sylvain Gallais, who has changed my life in beautiful ways, endless love.

CONTENTS

III

for Sylvain

THE INCOGNITO BODY

—And yet the things

That happen! Signs,
Promises—
                    George Oppen

                    I say across the waves of the air to you:
today once more
I will try to be non-violent
one more day
this morning, waking the world away
In the violent day.
                    —Muriel Rukeyser

Is this fair use, to find
            the intergown of difference
            severing self from = = nonself = = gone.
                    —Alice Fulton

I

At Delphi

The myth was all we had. That story,
but what was it? A path up a mountain,
and at the top, a rock, a tunnel
or entrance to an underground cave.

I could feel this . . . how to describe
a feeling that started like a vibration
or opening in the chest cavity,
then in the head and feet

even as I walked from the bottom
of the path and up, a winding
through thin pines lining the way?
The sun hailed us like song,

an old riming of light.
This was a road pilgrims
had traveled. We were walking it,
and my feet knew I walked here

before. They knew this way.
The feeling didn't fade
but grew stronger as we came
into a great cleft in the cliffs.

A guide said, This was the sibyl's rock,
and beside that precarious jut of boulder
was an opening into the ground.
I was vibrating like a divining rod.

There was nowhere to go
but through the ruins. My sister heard
a tone or tones, *A chord*, she said,
warning of peril or sorrow. A future

we could see but not change.
The story is the path or way.
We happen upon it once or twice,
arrive in the lucid noon

to a place where we once came
to know what we do not know.
My body knew. Still. It felt
like a feeling. I called it a feeling.

STONES

The universe is stone, but we are not.

—George Oppen

I have a friend who imprisons stones.
How do you do that? I ask.
I build little cages and put them in.
And why do you imprison these stones?
They are immoral stones. I oversee
the purification of petrified beings.
Where do you find these immoral stones?
I find them in the river,
which is low in the summer drought.
Are all the stones you see immoral?
No, only the ones I imprison.
Can you tell which stones are immoral?
Yes, I can tell which ones are immoral,
and which are not.
And where do you keep the cages?
I keep them on a shelf, near the window.
And do you keep them by the window
so they see their old abode
and know what they have lost?
I keep them by the window because
that is where I have room.
Will you free these stones?
Yes, when they have learned morality
and are purified of being petrified.
Will you teach them morality and courage?
No, morality and courage cannot be taught
but they can be learned.
How will imprisoned stones learn?
They will learn because I have moved them

and that is what they feared most.
When will they know they have learned?
I will know when they know.

Radical Optimism

I held the cup, which emptied.
Possibly I watched. I balanced
on a bench. The room chattered,

a party. I dashed notes:
Can you be with not knowing,
living the separation, cult.

of grief (culture or cultivation)?
A broken heart is a whole (I'd torn
it away). Grasped a filled cup.

Around me swirled laughter
as if the glimmering sprawl
of the Milky Way emerged

when wisps of clouds scuttled past
in the night's wind. I couldn't look
up. If outside, I'd not have

noticed. This lasted hours,
then morning came. The words
were clouds swept away

by laughter. I scribbled,
trying to preserve the invisible
ink of memory, and that breaking.

THE BOOK OF WHAT IS

At heart the book of what is,
call it "truth," "wave-
marbled water," "man,

walking down path,"
greeting you like an old
flame tempered by winters

the river froze and held
snow's weight, springs
when ice melted his icy heart

in hours (not years)
and the river's shell
opened, milky, chartreuse

with last summer's lichen, pine-
branches scattered among,
everything preserved, fresh-

seeming the small green needles
of memory, all that pungent
urgency there freed.

Four Ways of Seeing the Fall

1

The sleep of trees lies deep as dreams.
You rise in thought, everyone open-minded.
When you speak the sky reflects your words.
Sometimes the mellowness of autumn
makes you laugh. You're thoughtful or cruel,
but you can't tell the difference. In the garden,
the yellow hedges spread their lace of light.

2

The disorientation I felt passed quickly.
Not disoriented but disorigined;
I searched old notebooks, letters.
The street was empty, but I could hear others
in the alley where, last night, the dog
cornered something that huddled fat, furry
against the wall, the dog barking, even inside.

3

We passed the flame, one to another.
The frame of relation didn't hold,
its structure flawed. I looked outside
at an outside that would never be the same
in my perceptions, as if God had withdrawn,
undramatically. I rocked and huddled,
huddled and rocked. It was cold.

4

It is now. And now it is also now,
but not the same now. Now
is not now. To live with change

is like an empty pocket in which,
nevertheless, you find the ring
you had misplaced. Where was it when
you searched, and found nothing there?

Though We Change, One Flying after Another
after Virginia Woolf

In essence you embrace the real,
thinking to lift it to your face,
its fragrance like a moonflower
scenting the nights of no-moon.
A small object, detritus of a life
left behind, forgotten, of import
uncertain. What do you mean
when you say *I don't know?*

Dust rises after a storm,
trees tornadoed down, live wires
snaking through streets. Cities
track in census rolls
their growing miserables
who speak in dialect among themselves,
another country of expendable people:
not invisible enough; looked past.

Is life very solid or shifting?
This goes on forever, this moment
you stand on which is also
evanescent, diaphanous, flying.
It may be that though we change,
flying one after another, so quick,
so quick, we're somehow continuous we
human beings and show the light through.

What is the light? *Turn around*
a bird sings to you for no reason,
your hands splayed against a wall,
your face pushed against the wall.

You hear the echoing chambers within
the gun's rotating barrel, your life
a loaded gun. You have the power
to die. You are your neighbor's soul.

Modern Life

As to the future perfect, we begin with dynamic,
fluctuate verbs to soothsay desire's half-life
(the internal matters). The clearsighted seek
a prevalent truth in fact: rust telltaling on cars,
children's runny noses, a toddler shitting
in the clinic of a doctor who knows it's a sign
of distress. What can she do by which time
she'll have opened blinds to regard the infinite
rhododendron in bloom, in order turned her mind's
afterthought? Pruned and plucked. Not cross
but uncrossed. The city pearls in mist,
a park saves stones that lightning fired.
Her question stirs the palpable trace, the heart
of something gained. Though mere touchwood.

HONESTY

Demands scarcity? It's true,
pointing to "honesty-scarcity"
makes *sound* sense. Can you hear that?
The lilt of dactyls like didactic notes?
Such a rarity, verity, that we hoard its
compounding sweetness like Swiss chocolate

dollars squirreled away by addicts, misers
saving for later we're not sure why.
When I ask, Do you count? you say,
one by one (in the republic of dreams
there are many *you's* but no lies), "No. No one counts.
Don't you dance?" I too suddenly a *you*,

lining up to skirt issues and shift feet,
prevarication's oldest two-step, *yes-no, yes-no,*
crooning the *citoyen* blues. We're in the shallows,
multitudes of us, anonymous as the dear deer
gamboling freely beneath the susurrant leaves.
Trees wildly waving sparklers. Sound hollows.

INTERIOR

In the not-quite, an almost-turn
of events you leaven, as unkind
with kind,

saying "something's in the air,"
meaning nothing
irrevocable has happened yet

you won't say it won't
or what it is, that
said, distilling intent.

A soft whir of wings beyond
remembrance tells
you beauty—the phone

(muffled as if behind closed doors,   mother
no longer
home) rang and rang while in the attic

father bundled her clothes in silence,
and you had no memory for so long—
 defies despair,

that expanse you soar above,
as a car zooms up a valley
road toward noon.

It Is True That the True Appearance of an Object
—*after Robert Duncan*

Isn't perceptible, and in making-
up the seen we touch the truth? Curtains admit

the visible—call it simple—a fence, a tree
glimpsed through the lacy frame.

My neighbor is climbing a ladder
into the box elder in his backyard.

He talks to his wife below,
watching from the patio with a drink,

of (some) possible (thing).
He's sawing away all the branches

where evenings birds gathered by hundreds
loudly chirping unseen among the leaves

all summer as if the tree alone sang.
The branches, separated,

reassemble on the ground
where they fell. The tree is being

sawed down to stump
and rising beside itself.

With birds flown silence surge
wherever sentience

"declares the co-existence of real
and selves," wherein that divide

of our making what is
stands most revealed.

A Poem with Lines from Elytis' Eros, Eros, Eros

In love's countryside, houses no longer have roofs!
On the path toward sea, we peeked inside
the uncovered rooms like honeycombs.
We lay uncovered, too, on earth's hair.

Swans sang to us, their V for *vivre*,
the season so late. Against a weathered barn,
branches arc like winter runes I cannot read.
The future, inscrutable, holds us

to its unwritten account. Already we secret
the memory of our bodies together become
holographs of desire. *The briefest route
between two people*: ravishing script, mystery

of eros, its only philosophy (chloro-
phylled glyph of dream life) to infuse faith
with simplicity: above the azure plain,
a blue that shimmers, that shifts.

Memory Y

One spring I felt another realm.
Images surface like artifacts in a midden.
In a volcanic valley, lava dolmens
pierce the winter sky at dusk,

darkness in a darkening:
the Valley of Echoing Cliffs.
I walk to the ridge of basalt near a stream
and the fire we have built to cook.

I'm stopped short of that wall
as if by another. My hands circle
in air for an invisible entrance
I can perceive but not find.

High above, carved out in the cliff-face
is a huge cave called the Elf Cathedral.
I will dream of its bishop on a dais
with his rubied miter and staff,

and I in the congregation. This memory
is part of a story that fell away.
Water from the stream was so cold
the throat ached drinking. There was love-

making on the shore among the willows,
though there could not have been willows.

We see the mountain's summit mist,
a crown of silver streaks on black.
Our breath puffs and vanishes.
The moon cresting the peak

outlines the clouds in white from
behind.
                    Wait for Me.
We scatter like penitentes on
the steps of La Morada, the 19th-c.

sect of flagellants who still in places
choose each spring a "Christ" to bind
with rope in mock crucifixion.
                    Do not speak of them.

A large cross cuts the night sky,
reddening, a shifting glow
that deepens, fans into scarlet, etching
Taos Mountain with gossamers of

green. Clouds break.
                    Now you'll see.
The moon draws a glimmer Calvary
trail we follow through the high desert.

Pungency of sage, chaparral.
We find bear scat, or cat, marks of
Reeboks, then both Reeboks,
and beside them, crumpled jeans

as if someone, meaning in fact to
come back, had taken a dip into
thin air.

Nothing you see now.

THE SEEKER
after Tarkovsky's Stalker

I live on the zone's edge which we call The Forest.
Why? you ask. Why what? I ask back.

For my calling I crawl, vermin-like,
through a glade with a battalion of burnt
tanks, their guns every which-way, matchsticks.

A cast-iron stove simmers in a field of good intentions,
boils over under a clear sky when we pass. Up ahead,

Hope remains in the one intact room
left in a house overlooking the river valley.
I am taking you to fear's threshold. Who?

Anyone who asks. Rain curtains the room's entrance.
Elsewhere a phone rings. You

pick up the receiver, No,
this is not the maternity ward.
Now, it rains in the room itself,

water filling with fish that nose the oily, rainbowed swirls,
come from nowhere. You've walked to the archway,

pause to say: It's
raining in the room.
I say, I don't know the way out,

only the way in. My daughter when her big heart burst
stared so hard at the book, the glass, the hand-

painted pitcher of water on the table,
they shook as if the past hurtled nearby.
They inched toward her, moving, but she

was not moved. When the book fell open, she mouthed the
words,
not looking up. Not looking, really, for anything at all.

On the Way Was Found That

To sleep on the midnight
sheen the ferry
chugged through was to keep
waking askewed on benches like pews

in Tourist. To doze with the engine's
muffled rumble humming inside
as if life were growing there—
though life would never grow there—

was not to know the future or the past
beyond the self
yet to find it. Fluorescents effervescing
through hours paced like the heart,

the flickering stopped at last as a guard
roughed the prone bodies, one
girl then the other, sweeping their
feet to the floor, the force of gesture

narrated in gruff English, touch without feeling,
neither thinking of the other
as *having felt*. The sea's air filtered
the grainy pink light over a moving

azure plane, lifting, sinking, shaking
out the floating, blue-silk sheet. Dawn.
The boat crested to shore where marble
columns abut sky, where to climb

the sacred mountain was to herd up the hill's
narrowing path with others
clicking cameras, in many
tongues speaking. There to descend by broken

jagging stairs. At the bottom would be,
you said, shivering suddenly under sun,
a small, roofless room, or courtyard
with a few mosaics still intact,

one the bleached-out form
of a crouching leopard, but turning to look back,
not pouncing, you said, and its snarl
perhaps in warning, perhaps in fear.

II

The Incognito Body

> Physical pain does not simply resist language but actively destroys it, bringing about an immediate reversion to . . . the sounds and cries a human being makes before language is learned.
> —Elaine Scarry

> For that is one property of poetic language: to engage with states that themselves would deprive us of language and reduce us to passive sufferers.
> —Adrienne Rich

1. In another country

Wake to breeze and satin-
sheen of blue past
village clattered
up since gale-force
winds flattened it

With slow, slug-
moves (gray-
pouched skin), I

> more contemptible: since ours is to preserve
> arthewormes: didst thou ever see a Larke in a
> cage? such is the soule in the body. . . .

limp to this shore,
stand in white
light on white sand,
step into sea

so salty that
I float free
        of gravity

2. The Hour of Lead

All fall I waited (in a high tide
of pain: neck, toes, knees, fingers
stiffening, unmovable) for
joint damage. Climbed one stair
at a time. Pain I tried to ignore
became fact; bearing it made
the days "good" or "bad." Sometimes
with a shock of pain and sometimes
with a dream I could not dream
of sleep. This body I knew
not, wanted not, was not a dream,
nor a trapped-inside-of fate
that leaves as it came, rolling back,
a tide going out when I wake.

3. The Nerves like Tombs

As if an island under fog, memory's
outline blurs in fall and disappears
in spring. A broken chrysalis, the soul
dries up, self-emptied. When I
drive through town, I do not see
a stop light that I hurtle (deadly)
past to find myself crossing the river
out of town. I don't know why I stutter,
or sentence stops and words like crows
wheel, cawing, away. One fears
for a self, but I have no fears
for this no-more being, this body-shell
with nothing-left to say. *First chill,
then stupor. Then the letting go.*

4. BODY SCANS

Almost comforting, cradling &
claustrophobic, the metal
tunnel surrounds you
with driving sound, head strapped
down so nothing moves. A voice
floats through the little mike:
"All right in there? Are you still
all right?" You're told half
an hour but it's fifty minutes.
Cold, you're hurtling
in space toward Mars,
chanting though you know
they hear you as they scan
your brain, deeper than the sea
& differing from God
as syllable from sound.
Later, when you huddle
on a table, they place
your feet, hands on a graph,
take pictures to see you
through & through.
Light cast from above
the machine marks
you with a cross,
a slanted star, a stained
glass window of a church.
"Don't breathe," they call,
                      & you don't.

5. Much that you don't remember

All dreams

To recOVER is nOt
to change
an experience of separation
a decreasing capacity
to find wORDs

> You were gOing to say
> Could think of nOthing to say
> Had sOmething to say
> and suddenly after a sentence

>> lose language

Sometimes cOMplete   withdRAW
no sexual
no touch

was to flOat
without gravity
emptied Out until
nO "I" left
tO act human
gONE

> *As art this SHATTERing*
> *can disPLAY the prO*
>> *ductive basis*
> *of subJEctIve and iDEO*

50

lOgical sig-
nIFying FORMations

nEVER cOMe back

6. Since you cannot think

There are LESSons here—
humility, de-
tachMEnt from ambI-
                    shuns—
                    wORld-
ly not spirIT-
                ual: how else can one
who has felt whOle
accept the still i-
MAGInation, the VITAl EVEning:

        moving
        un-
able

favoring my left
wrist has erupted) YESterday
for the rest of the day, in-
crEASING   By evening
FULLy affected

> Attempts have been made to evaluate
> physical, emotional, and social well being.
> Patients score high on tests designed to
> reveal hypochondriasis, depression, hysteria
> and sexual aversion, but low on tests
> designed to measure self-esteem.

beCAUSE so
far, (ex-
cept for mOrnings)
to walk with
pain   not
know what will
learn to stay
tendering the tENDer

                      pARTs

They don't know
what you have and you have
to keep lEARNing/ re-

                      MINDing

to cultivate all winter

                      Patience

You are "blank,"
not tHERE
not the self
not the laugh with

                      not the drive to NY

not your wILL

> The person with chronic illness is unable to
> escape the intense experiencing of social
> strain (guilt, resentment, frustration),
> through projection, displacement, repression
> or sublimation, but the disease also invites
> her to attack social stress at its source.

To be aLIVE in the smALLest

                          very simple
THINGS

little left
to dream—
to wish for

no
                    consciousness   of anything
but WILD   and unsavory
        sadness

to see what it hOLDs
from fear so often from
rAGErage

7. Green surrounds the mind of summer—

Taking time, patience
This new body a new land
The doctor said, "Let's say
that people with green haIr
are more likely to cOntract
this disease, so for our purposes
it's as if you have green haIr."
He wOn't kill
but he cannot

                          cure you

There is nO cure
Now there's nO there

          your mind left
          without your body
          Where did "you"
          gO?

> The study of individual illness, with the
> notion of **social illness**, is a window for us
> to look at the characteristics of social experi-
> ence in our society, as well as the develop-
> ment, maintenance and treatment of disease.

This happens dAILy
This unspecified this, a waking
and thinking This Is It this!
Take it, beLIEve this is
not in your control
You do not read about this

                                        "isn't news"

If nothing means anything
the medical report
a construction of meaning
to mean something

> The paradigm of the **healthy social world
> of normal people** sees social support
> therapy as a rite of passage. The person
> with chronic illness is cast into a
> permanent liminal state.

then *disease-free*
is a state of being
you can claim
to emBODY, saying if
you do, you do, and you dO
(it's a lie)

8. The Exhibit of Pain

In the Blue Gallery:

> Chronic patients exaggerate personal
> disability and **unfortunate event**,
> triggering unnecessary sympathetic
> arousal, feelings of anxiety, and tonic
> **changes** in muscles.

In the Gray Gallery:

> The fortune tellers' error constitutes
> **hopelessness**, the belief in an indefinite
> continuation of pain and misfortune.

In the Red Gallery:

> Confusing **desire** for pleasure with a **need**
> for pleasure is a self-defeating position:
> that one must give in to short-term
> **pleasure**.

In the Yellow Gallery:

Overgeneralization causes **depression**. "Many of us believe that our worth as humans depends upon how well we perform." Patients **denigrate** their worth when they cannot function at premorbit levels, i.e. cannot work.

In the Magic Gallery:

Through their illness, patients are invited to **redress** social commitments and broken promises by addressing their conscience. They discover possibilities for **restoration**.

9. A SEASON OF PAIN

A sentence lasting all
year, then another in present
perfect: am having pain

        Sentences, raked
        into small shames
        like so many piles of leaves
        The phenomenon of any-
        body, in essence a-
        mazing, stops
        you cold

Take my body, your friend remarks
The rounded hips, overflowing breasts
of another era's *maternal*
is such comfort with her cream soups,
homemade breads: *Motherly*
Mother, mother
this soul's dark night

        —Es of essence
        Chant of enchantment

Your friend laughs
The laughter runs over you
You laugh too
until you cannot
help yourself

Say: *Even unto the end,*
lo, I am with you always

Driving home you do not see
deer in brush beside the road
When they spring
suddenly away you
stop amazed to
watch them bound

10. She forecast the future

Los Angeles, summers ago. Blue whales returning to the California coast, following the plankton washed north from Mexico by warm winds. Hundreds of leaping bottlenose dolphins with their young, humpbacks spouting in the distance, orcas, and three of the largest mammal on earth, the blue whale.

One with a scarred fin trolled alongside us, dis/playing himself, so close that he could have flipped the boat. He'd arc sideways and dive past the hull, his great fluke reaching straight into the air. Then he'd turn around and do the whole display again. We shared him with another boat for an hour, the whale crisscrossing between us. The captain insisted he'd never seen anything like it in twenty years of sailing.

Our tickets were a gift from my sister, a news producer who'd been out the day before with a crew filming a few spouts in the distance. Her boat was filled with children who kept stealing the camera man's equipment. It had been very rough. Everyone got sick.

The sea was calm for us. We felt the joy in our bones. In the evening, my friend Anna read my cards: *after much hardship, a great gift.*

11. Among Pain

For the body possibly to have gone through,
of the minutest and crucial sensations,
each having its purpose, or configuration:
In the mind everything goes, larger than sky
or God, the heft of all being in perception,

the weight of weight, of sense the same
only through feelings everyone shares:
"I" does not seem unbelievable nor events improbable.
Pain bleeds through imagination, unimaginative:
it just is. One wishes to do something, go somewhere,

but everywhere the sensation remains,
the body in pain. Its eyes look
on fuchsia and lilac overtaking
the back fence, it still bleeds,
and I am knowing this

(body that cannot rise
from its chair,
that never weeps,
in earth's house—
hold of pain).

My mind scrolls through a list of disappeared,
decimated beings. If there is no escape,
no separation, there are also no lies.
Sun shines on the arid soil of this garden.
Pain blooms in a body. Blossoms without water.

12. In a Mute Season

Questions rail along the field
where winter wheat lies hidden
in snow. (We lie to justify
indefensible behavior, to protect
unprotectable innocence, inhaling
and exhaling with an evenness
of spirit to which we aspire.)
Who calls the sky gray?
or the seasons from hell?

I visit doctors because
my body drives me to them,
beyond my dictates. Ailing,
I am healing before
my mind understands
that the phenomenology of pain
harbors words which refuse
syntax and order, predictable,
eventual inevitability,

until I grasp that order
eludes us, dispersing,
a wall of fog we drive through,
so frugal of speed, spendthrifts
of time. To feel alone is merely
the mind's last defense—
a physiological white-out—
from the spirit's largesse.

13. MY BODY IN DREAM-LANGUAGE

> *Because we don't know when we will die*
> *we get to think of life as an inexhaustible wealth.*
> —Paul Bowles

I'm riding a horse (for a last time?).
Something is wrong or "wrong."
Forbidden to ride I somehow
gallop on cobblestones.

> *Yet everything happens*
> *only a certain number of times,*
> *and only a small number really.*

I'm too high on the horse's neck
(it is my own horse I ride,
and the manor where we are
I also own, or owned).

> *How many more times will you remember*
> *a childhood afternoon, so deeply*
> *a part of your being you cannot*
> *conceive of life without it?*

I hold the reins too tight.
The horse stumbles.
We start to fall.

> *Perhaps four or five? How many*
> *more times watch the full moon rise?*
> *Yet it all seemed so limitless.*

But we do not fall.

III

Have We After All Come To

This? As if sunlight cast upon streets
auras of message or vision. Like oracles
the unsightly line up, parading
agony's mask. How spell indifference?
Give it a break?
                    Who have wasted our lives?

I glimpse foxfire in town,
where the square clangs with bells cut
from silence, ringing *out*
of time. I like a sound that's true,

but tell me we haven't lost
our circumference, that intimation
of wholeness, or erased
intuition from ken.

Far from the still center, touch
a lustrous stone for luck.
Look at the pool of sky in its depths,
the wavering trees, the shining
visage in its waters.

Elemental Attention. Stillness.

The backyard's birch scuffed
with scars of lopped branches
grows an inch a year,
       a totem of lament in winter, of hope's
       scatter of green this spring. How
       choose between these sentiments? Why?
If the question is asked,
must it then be answered
with a look of blank incomprehension
       or not at all? Here's reality's rub,
       that we don't feel its scrape
       until the bone shows through—

so bright, its never-healing,
as to entrance us. We're aware
the heart beats despite us,
       the mind's cacophony never rests
       and serendipity is earned, when one says:
       Enlightenment is an accident.
       Practice makes one accident-prone.

Like five-year-olds learning to bike,
we fall, skin knees, look askance.
These are not the accidents
       you had in mind? Are told:
       But I had nothing in mind.

ONCE UPON A TIME

The story you tell
grows blurred by repetition,
the child to whom you tell it fallen asleep.

You bored her.
How does that feel
to claim rights to the story, b/c

you earned it
like a salary, while the child
woke up, individuated, left as you slept

tangled in sheets
& dreams? You directed
something. Your team worked along

a stream's muddy
bank near a mansion. *Time*
wanted your picture. You mattered

at the moment
& spoke to the mansion's owner
about the great work your team had done,

how they, too,
should be in the picture.
You couldn't have been happier, or less sure

what anyone wished
to know. The ivy-covered stone
of the great house rose behind the owner

striding toward
the stream where you waited,
words flown. Your story happened so long ago.

No one thought it
mattered anymore, but that
wasn't ever what you meant. No never.

Late Nights with Albert

When I ask how the Theory
of Relativity came to him
Albert says, *In dreams.*

In dreams he understood
that our dance with an atom
was the last waltz.

What a Schadenfreude, *this waltz,*
Albert sighs when I wake him
from his wide-eyed trance.

So absent-minded with
his visions he'd become,
he lost sight of outcomes

or, I sometimes say, ignored
the details. *There's no time,*
he jots. Countless others

now dream of being
spacy as molecules
of Himalayan oxygen,

too hip to remember
the first to reach the summit
fell—lying unfound for years.

Oh, Albert, why did you
dream *so much?* I ask.
It was only the end

of matter, not an end
to the *matter*, wasn't it?
he cries softly to himself,

for the worst who join
nuclear to energy at a profit
and think a good day's

job incorporates
that neat quantity
into their kids' bodies

as if into portfolios.
Once *folios* imaged things
in the world: leaves

like wings aflutter in fall's
foliage reminding some scribe
of illumination.

Albert's dream breaks off
in showers of missteps
that finish the dance he began

and ends alone, spinning slowly
beneath the bursts of dumb stars
illumining the night.

Resurrection Is a Sense of Direction
—after a line from H.D.

At century's turn, the general discovers
he's obsolete, due for recall.
He clips his tatter of a moustache,
irons the uniform—also raggedy, musty.
He dreams of stars, a milky way
of decorations across his chest, and a brass band
cymbals clashing as he walks down the aisle
to be honored, saluting no one in particular,
the mirror, his darkened pane,

washed clean by last night's rain.
He'll start a war on Tuesday,
dissolve it into various skirmishes
by Friday, yell at the President
for pursuing a treaty, 100 times in the week
without recourse to the outside world. Where
has all his power gone? Why
does he think he commands anything

anymore? He lets go, go go
the things he lived for
with no thought of duty or regret,
to walk about those cavernous halls
where he dwells, selecting an apple
from one of the many decorative fruit bowls,
tasting its sweetness inside
the bitter shiny surface, ready
to chuck the core onto a track

he called My Life and make a dash for it,
having waited years for the dawning
of simple affirmation, a statue
cast to the god of resurgence,
greening with age: now the quick,
new buds opening, sprouting from his cane
as from a living staff, encompass him
and at last, he does not hesitate.

HIGH TEA AT VIRGINIA'S

Having written the letters all afternoon,
her desk overlooking a gentle verdancy,
the valley's breeze tufting her hair,
lifting its wisps at times into air, she'll brush
out the skirt she clutched so hard in thought
it crushed. She thinks now, too, walking by
the hollyhock and foxglove, "the voluptuous
purple, the creamy, waxen flesh: *Quelle âme
est sans défauts?*" She notes how swallows
whorl late summer's evening clouds, too soon
too chill to open windows wide, and growing
shadows shadows as light dims. On the eve
of war, Virginia, sipping tea like hemlock,
loves how the curtains billow. How they part.

ELEGY
          —for *Agha Shahid Ali* (1949-2001)

I searched a noon among Northampton's lawns
to find where death had hidden you.
You would have sighed, *So much green*,
preferring the towering concrete of New

York (less tall since you died) save for the blue
Himalayas of Kashmir. By 9/11
your memory was gone: you never knew.
Your grave shocked with pink carnations,

just a simple marker, and from it the white
wing of your poem—in windless air—
rose until a moment I thought you *there*
and so to read, or pray, I knelt.

When last we met you hugged so hard,
so hard, to tell me Daniel's name
again, him mine. And I, to hold your living hand,
sat close. You whispered, *No more poems*.

This fall instead I'll dance. O Shahid,
save me one, I said, when everything *you* was
being wrung, a distillate of love expressed,
that fall your dances ended.

The Sibyl's Spring (1999)

Today the lilacs bud,
their tight purple clusters
opening to plush lavender.

Winter's first refugees
fled the latest war while
here, the dogwood and cherry

flowered. When Apollo overcame
Earth, he stole her temple
at Delphi, making her python

his own. Today we call
earth's breath after her,
Gaia—all life part of that

inspiration, expiration. The bodies
of sons and young fathers
were planted together this spring

in the unplanted fields of Kosovo.
Now, dandelions grow beside hyacinths
in our garden and the wisteria

that you pruned before you left
will not bloom. The Delphic oracle
wasn't the pythoness drugged

and raving from the sibyl's rock
but the priests who translated her.
Time's survivors,

we must teach ourselves
a new language, simple
words with which to start—

hand, wood, balm—
for a time we won't
recall or dream.

Till I Have Conquered in Myself What Causes War (2000)
—after a line by Marianne Moore

acknowledging is—when
that
wasn't what was asked—
                              —Leslie Scalapino

In *Raising the Ashes*
the documentary montage of now
and then—"Ourself –
behind Ourself" – wasn't

acknowledged though a woman said,
"Faced with genocide, 99% of us
would kill them
to survive ourselves,"

those selves
not surviving
as they were
but had become,

crying, when asked
to admit this, *We knew*
nothing and will not bear
your ashen blame.

In Distrust of Good (2001)

—with a line by Wallace Stevens

A mind reasoning the good
in violence isn't a good. Truth
wanders through its waving fields

of untruths, all alike grown tall
in the rich soil. "Who's good?"
"Whose good?" the dead call beneath
gray trees with shorn branches.

An empty street, a dark house,
still, as if raided, and the life within
fled. The mind harboring

vengeance slips out of season,
heart's munificent rule.
The good is evil's last invention.
It casts aspersions like stones.

THAT WILD CHANCE OF LIVING (2001)

> Death in us goes on
> testing the wild
> chance of living.
> —Denise Levertov

This morning we hear the air
of Los Alamos is uranium-
laced. Harmless amounts,
a reporter reports. Wind
tests the currents as we drive
past, chancing to live here
and not there: As in Salgado's
"Human Migrations," light-
filled photos of all the places
where death has gone on and
on of good people on good
days, as Lakota and Apache
once said, to die, riding
to fight the whites, that history

flawing the tranquil town surface
with ghosts, spirits, sounds from
another time's *real* we can sense.
I called the angels by name,
H.D. wrote of the Blitz—
Uriel, Annael, Angel of Death,
Angel of Peace. At the Saint
Geronimo (*Michael*) dances
lightning flickered in the distance.
A young Coyote whirled from the circle
of Clowns to climb the tall pole
raised in the pueblo's center,

a flag caught on his belt
like an irreverent loincloth.

On top the pole, the dancer
slowly turned, holding
the flag whipping in wind rising
as rain came. *Did you know each one
of our nation's symbols is from war?*
my friend whispered. Thunder
clouds hid Taos Mountain,
the crowd humming when sun broke

       through and two
spectral arches   irradiant color-

       struck above the
eye watching   the war begin

Shame (2002)

We were all in line, all of us alike
                then not

alike. Some of the men were taken (few
                women),

made to hold this leg up then that, unzip
                and zip,

off and on. So thoroughly frisked one man
                joked (forced),

Whatever gives you kicks; then, *You people*
                get off

on this stuff, you perverts?; then, *You stupid*
                mother-

fuck, outrage roaring at the guard who stayed
                polite

            —

regardless. But not me, not hearing, then
                hearing

the rising voice, and words that poked the mind's
                edge like

pins stuck into the breaking flesh of a-
                wareness.

I looked at him while pulling boots back on,
                Better

than being blown up, isn't it? Thank you!
                the guards

gathered around me. Maybe someone else
                speaking

meant: We're caught together in this warp

                                        of time

having less to do with danger than with

                                        power

that none of us on either side of the

                                        coach class

security line actually had.

                        ~

Or maybe not.
        The words cre-
                ating a
                        vacuum a-
                                mong us locked
                                          tight our breath.

                        ~

Small eyes behind thick glasses. Blinked under

                                        blinding

fluorescents as if too long in darkness.

                                        The man

disheveled everywhere—his khakis' zipper

                                        down, belt

off, buttoned-down shirt unbuttoned, blazer

                                        awry.

When his children (7 and 9?), watching

84

father

become stranger, fuming at strangers,

tugged him

away, I turned to the guard, *You have a*

very

hard job. All along I'd tried to—know how

to—speak

through words dividing—separating—us.

The guard

shook his inscrutable head, *It's gonna*

be just

fine. *I'm always fine!* He heard and swiveled

round ex-

ploding in my face, *Bitch!* (the urge to strike

spittled

through the curse). Close up, he looked so like an

aging

Harry Potter, at first I marveled at

his dis-

play, more astonished than afraid. His chil-

dren rushed

in front of him, their mouths in O's of *Stop*

it! *Stop*

it, Daddy! He didn't mean it! We're so

sorry!

～

It's all right I hushed, at last to notice

bodies

trembled in shocked air atoms cracked open

ions

hurtling toward the cosmos of others

to what

end when fury spread particulate to

his wife

waiting down the hall as their children

bleated

back and forth between? I walked past feeling

silly

not looking, nor holding my head up when

she screamed

How much shame must we endure in one day

from you?

86

a still volcano Life holds his.   peace.
he casts spells about like scattered. prayers:
may excess temper and mettle the bitter. expel.
Camus once wrote that love must.   permeate.

all we do. to complicate life with.   reflection.
among a field of psalms one dawn he. *sang,*
horizon to become a line of gold from. grove.
to house. then the glowing open: a: gape.

we climbed the canyon and she spoke of spirit.
a gash. a bleeding into the ground. *of blood*
merged with earthwound: a joining. boulders
bordered the trail. light incandesced. wind
flecked with juniper. amaranth-seed. lavender.
clouds framing the Gorge like blinds drawn:
to see Orion Ursa Major Cassiopeia orient
the town in darkness. that sharp scent was sage.

certain of your habits to which I.   surrender, a river.
cranes in silhouette. one-legged sentinels. *a wake:*
I was last night the heart in its nest beating

fast beating. breathing, and with grace cradling.
thoughts of. tattered bits. velvet vaunting the wild:
nerves surged, *nor dream.* the brittle: crackle.

fear-shards. of scoring skin (nor scarring): *souls*
together clasp: a continuously jeopardized.
a feeling that love is: not anonymous not dead.

Notes

I

"Radical Optimism": The term is what Buddhists call the capacity to live with
indeterminacy. Italicized portions are quoted from notes on a talk on Buddhism
by Joan Halifax, Roshi, at Omega Institute (August 1999, New York).

"Though We Change, One Flying after Another": title and collaged and intention-
ally misquoted portions of third and fourth strophes are from Virginia Woolf's
Moments of Being.

"Modern Life" is for Dr. Marion Brown.

"It Is True That the True Appearance of an Object": Title and quoted line from a
letter of Robert Duncan to H.D., 15 August 1959 (which also appear in his "After
Reading H.D.'s *Hermetic Definitions*").

"Seeing the Northern Lights on Taos Mesa" is for Fetzer Mills, Jr. and Michael
Knight.

II: "The Incognito Body"

Epigraphs: from Elaine Scarry's *The Body in Pain* and Adrienne Rich's "Voices from
the air."

Part 1
***portion in italics from *The Duchess of Malfi* (also embedded in quotation in Rich's
essay, "Voices from the air").

Part 5
***portion in italics quoted from Julia Kristeva's *Revolution in Poetic Language*.

Parts 6, 7, 8
***Indented and framed medical discourse excerpted from an unpublished article entitled "Experiencing Health with Rheumatoid Arthritis: An Anthropological Study of Illness, Treatment and Cure," by Jón Haukur Ingimundarson, Ph.D. (quoted with permission).

Part 13
 ***Italicized portions spoken by Paul Bowles in Bernardo Bertolucci's *The Sheltering Sky* (after Bowles's novel of the same title; quoted lines are from the film version).

III:
"Elemental Attention. Stillness": Italicized portion from a talk on Buddhism by Joan Halifax, Roshi, at Omega Institute (August 2000, New York).

"Till I Have Conquered in Myself What Causes War" takes its title from a line by Marianne Moore. My thanks to Lynne Schweizer for help in writing this poem.

"In Distrust of Good": my thanks to Jacqueline Vaught Brogan for reminding me of this line from Stevens.

"That Wild Chance of Living" is for Magdalene Smith and Barbara Kingsolver.

 "psalm: at the retreat house" is for Rick Givens.

"psalm: after hiking reading the stars" is for Roz Driscoll and Wendy Fidao.

BIOGRAPHICAL NOTE

Cynthia Hogue was born in the Midwest and raised in the Adirondack Mountains of upstate New York. After graduating from Oberlin College, she completed her Masters in Arts and Humanities (later the Buffalo Poetics Program) at SUNY/Buffalo, and received a Fulbright Fellowship to Iceland, where she lived and taught at the University of Iceland for three years. After returning to the States, Hogue completed a Ph.D. at the University of Arizona, in Tucson. She taught in the MFA program at the University of New Orleans before moving to Pennsylvania, where she directed the Stadler Center for Poetry at Bucknell University for eight years. She currently lives in Arizona with her husband, the French economist Sylvain Gallais, where she is the Maxine and Jonathan Marshall Chair in Modern and Contemporary Poetry in the Department of English at Arizona State University. While in Pennsylvania, she trained in conflict resolution with the Mennonites and became a trained mediator specializing in diversity issues in education. Among her honors are a National Endowment for the Arts Fellowship, an NEH Summer Seminar Fellowship, and the H.D. Fellowship at the Beinecke Library at Yale University. Her other collections are *Flux* (2002), *The Never Wife* (1999), *The Woman in Red* (1990), and *Where the Parallels Cross* (1984). Her critical work includes the co-edited *We Who Love To Be Astonished: Experimental Feminist Poetics and Performance Art*, the forthcoming first edition of H.D.'s *The Sword Went Out to Sea*, and the forthcoming *In Her Words: Contemporary Innovative Women Poets (Works and Interviews)*, both co-edited.

Printed in the USA
CPSIA information can be obtained
at www.ICGtesting.com
JSHW082223140824
68134JS00015B/709